GENERATION CODE

I'M AN HTML
WEB PAGE BUILDER

{ BUILD 12 PROGRAMS }

HTML

5

Max Wainewright
Crabtree Publishing Company
www.crabtreebooks.com

Crabtree Publishing Company
www.crabtreebooks.com
1-800-387-7650

Published in Canada
Crabtree Publishing
616 Welland Avenue
St. Catharines, ON
L2M 5V6

Published in the United States
Crabtree Publishing
PMB 59051
350 Fifth Ave, 59th Floor
New York, NY 10118

Published in 2018 by CRABTREE PUBLISHING COMPANY.

First published in 2017 by Wayland
Text copyright © ICT Apps Ltd, 2017
Art and design copyright © Hodder and Stoughton Limited, 2017

Author: Max Wainewright
Editorial director: Kathy Middleton
Editors: Catherine Brereton, Janine Deschenes
Freelance editor: Hayley Fairhead
Designer: Peter Clayman
Illustrator: Maria Cox
Proofreader: Wendy Scavuzzo
Prepress technician: Tammy McGarr
Print and production coordinator: Margaret Amy Salter

Consultant: Lee Martin, B. Ed, E-Learning Specialist

The website addresses (URLs) included in this book were valid at the time of going to press. However, it is possible that contents or addresses may have changed since the publication of this book. No responsibility for any such changes can be accepted by either the author or the Publisher.

E-safety
Children will need access to the Internet for most of the activities in this book. Parents or teachers should supervise this and discuss staying safe online with children.

Printed in the USA/072017/CG20170524

Library and Archives Canada Cataloguing in Publication

Wainewright, Max, author
      I'm an HTML web page builder / Max Wainewright.

(Generation code)
Includes index.
Issued in print and electronic formats.
ISBN 978-0-7787-3516-8 (hardcover).--ISBN 978-0-7787-3530-4 (softcover).--
ISBN978-1-4271-1936-0 (HTML)

      1. HTML (Document markup language)--Juvenile literature. 2. Web sites--Design--Juvenile literature. I. Title. II. Title: I am an HTML web page builder.

QA76.76.H94W37 2017   j006.7'4   C2017-902529-5
                                                C2017-902530-9

Library of Congress Cataloging-in-Publication Data

CIP available at the Library of Congress

CONTENTS

 RESPECTING COPYRIGHT

Copyright means the legal ownership of something. You need to think about who owns the images or sound files you are linking to or downloading in your apps. There shouldn't be any major issues unless you try to make an app available to the public. Check with an adult to make sure.

An alternative is to find a free-to-use image or sound file. Search for an image or sound, then look for the **Settings** button on the website results page. Click **Advanced search**, then look for **usage rights**. On that menu, choose **free to use share or modify, even commercially**.

INTRODUCTION

In this book, you will learn how to code your own amazing web pages using *HTML*. HTML stands for Hypertext Markup Language. It is the language used to build web pages. The programs in this book use version 5 of HTML (HTML5). You'll find out how to add text, images, *links*, and even videos to a web page. Once you have completed every program, you will be on your way to becoming an HTML expert!

There are many different tools you can use to build web pages:

You could use a simple *text editor*—a program that lets you enter, change, and store text.

Simple text editors work fine, but can be touchy. This is because the software won't help you.

```
page.html
1  <html>
2  <p>My text</p>
```

supereasywebbuilder.com
My website

There are many Internet sites and blogging tools that are able to quickly build web pages, but using these doesn't teach you about HTML.

The best thing to use for the activities in this book is an offline HTML editor, such as Sublime Text. This will support you as you type your code, but also give you the opportunity to learn the actual HTML code.

There are two separate windows that you'll be using:

```
Sublime Text
1  <html>
2    <h1>The Forest</h1>
3    <img src='tree.jpg'>
4  </html>
```

The **text editor** to make your HTML page.

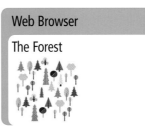

Web Browser
The Forest

The *browser* to view your HTML page.

Read through each page of this book, then try the activities. You'll learn how to put the basic elements on a web page, then add different colors and font sizes. Toward the end of the book, you'll be able to do some amazing programs and even create your own mini-websites.

Note: Words in *italics* appear in the glossary on page 30.

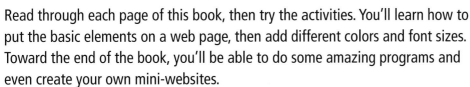

› GETTING STARTED

There are lots of ways to create an HTML file. There will probably be a simple text editor already on your computer called Notepad (if you have Windows), or TextEdit (on a Mac). These programs can help you get started, but it will be easier to create HTML if you download a more powerful text editor. In this book, we will use a text editor called Sublime Text. There are many other text editors you could download, such as Brackets or Notepad++. All of these are free for you to try out.

STEP 1 – FIND THE SUBLIME TEXT WEBSITE ▷

⇨ Open your web browser and visit **www.sublimetext.com**.

www.sublimetext.com

STEP 2 – START DOWNLOADING ▷

⇨ Click the **Download** button near the top of the web page.

Download

⇨ Choose which version you need. If you are not sure, then ask an adult to help you. To find your computer system on a Mac, click the Apple menu, then **About**. On a PC, click the **Start** menu, select **System**, and click **About**.

⇨ Wait for the download to complete.

STEP 3 – INSTALL THE SOFTWARE ▷

⇨ Some web browsers will then ask you to run the installation program. Choose **Run**.

⇨ If this does not happen, don't panic. The installer file should have been downloaded to your computer.

Look in your **Downloads** folder for it. Double-click the file to start installing your new text editor. You should get a big gray box giving you instructions about what to do next. Follow these instructions to complete the installation.

WHY DO WE NEED HTML?

There are more than 600 million active web pages in the world. HTML is the universal language that is used to create all of these web pages.

A special program called a browser is used to view a web page. Commonly used browsers include Chrome, Internet Explorer, Safari, and Firefox.

HTML pages can contain different things, including text, graphics, tables, headings, buttons, links, and videos. Each of these separate things is called an *element*.

Each element has tags and content. The tag explains what type of element to display and the content tells the browser what to display inside that element.

STEP 4 – RUN SUBLIME TEXT

On a PC:

⇨ Click **Start > Programs > Sublime Text.** Or just click **Sublime Text** if it appears in the **recently added** section.

On a Mac:

⇨ Click **Finder.**

⇨ Click **Applications.**

Applications

⇨ Make a shortcut by dragging **Sublime Text** from **Finder** onto your dock at the bottom of the **Desktop.**

⇨ Click the **Sublime Text** icon.

STEP 5 – YOUR FIRST PAGE

⇨ Carefully type this into your text editor for lines 1, 2, and 3:

Sublime Text

1 <html>
2 <p>Welcome</p>
3 </html>

Start all HTML files with <html>.

Show a paragraph saying Welcome.

End all HTML files with </html>.

STEP 6 – SAVE YOUR PAGE

⇨ Click **File** > **Save.**

⇨ Save to your *Documents folder*.

⇨ Type **welcome.html** as the filename.

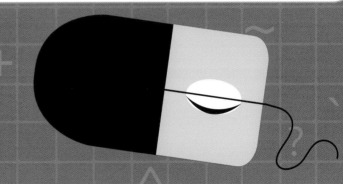

STEP 7 – VIEW YOUR PAGE

⇨ Open your **Documents** folder.

⇨ Find the **welcome.html** file and double-click it.

 Your very first web page should now load in your normal web browser! It should look something like this:

Documents/welcome.html

Welcome

TAGS

KEY CONCEPT

- *Tags* always start with **<** and end with **>**. These are known as angle brackets.

- All elements have an **opening tag.** Most also have a **closing tag.**

Opening tag   Closing tag

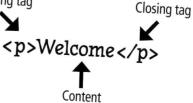

<p>Welcome</p>

Content

❯ HEADINGS AND PARAGRAPHS

Now that you know how to make a very simple HTML web page, let's experiment and add some other elements to the page. We'll start by looking at how to add special text elements called headings.

STEP 1 – START YOUR TEXT EDITOR

On a PC:

⇨ Click **Start > Programs > Sublime Text.**

On a Mac:

⇨ Click the **Sublime Text** icon.

STEP 2 – ENTER THIS HTML

⇨ Carefully type this into your text editor for lines 1 to 6:

Sublime Text

1	`<html>`	Start the web page.
2	`<h1>My Timetable</h1>`	Add main heading.
3	`<p>Math</p>`	Add first paragraph.
4	`<p>English</p>`	Add second paragraph.
5	`<p>Science</p>`	Add third paragraph.
6	`</html>`	End the web page.

STEP 3 – SAVE YOUR PAGE

⇨ Click **File** > **Save**.

⇨ Save to your **Documents** folder.

⇨ Type **timetable.html** as the filename.

STEP 4 – VIEW YOUR PAGE

⇨ Open your **Documents** folder.

⇨ Find the **timetable.html** file and double-click it.

⇨ Your web page should now load in your browser.

⇨ Notice how the **<h1>** heading tag has made the heading text large and bold.

Documents/timetable.html

My Timetable
Math
English
Science

STEP 5 – ARRANGE YOUR SCREEN

As you start to develop more complex HTML pages, you need to be able to see the code and the HTML page at the same time.

⇨ Resize your text editor and browser windows so your screen looks like this whenever you are working on programs in HTML:

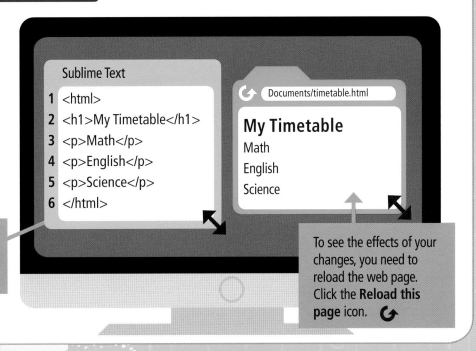

Sublime Text

```
1  <html>
2  <h1>My Timetable</h1>
3  <p>Math</p>
4  <p>English</p>
5  <p>Science</p>
6  </html>
```

Documents/timetable.html

My Timetable
Math
English
Science

If you make a change to your HTML in the text editor, save your file.

To see the effects of your changes, you need to reload the web page. Click the **Reload this page** icon.

CUSTOMIZE

- Change the timetable so it matches your own.

- Add to the timetable so it includes every day of the week.

- Experiment with other heading tags, from **<h1>** down to **<h6>**.

- Remember to use closing tags, too: **</h6>**.

STEP 6 – SUBHEADINGS

⇨ Change your code so it has **subheadings** for Monday and Tuesday:

Sublime Text

```
1  <html>
2  <h1>My Timetable</h1>
3  <h3>Monday</h3>
4  <p>Math</p>
5  <p>English</p>
6  <h3>Tuesday</h3>
7  <p>Science</p>
8  <p>History</p>
9  </html>
```

Insert an **<h3>** subheading that says **Monday**. Don't forget the closing tag **</h3>**. When you add the / in the closing tag, most editors will finish the tag for you.

Add another **<h3>** element for **Tuesday**. Close it with the tag **</h3>**.

Add more paragraphs to show other subjects.

 Now view your new web page!

KEY CONCEPT

HEADINGS

- Use **<h1>** and **</h1>** tags to show important headings on your pages. Use other tags, such as **<h3>**, for less significant headings.

› A TOUCH OF COLOR

Color can be very useful as a way of drawing people's attention to different things on your web page. Color can also help explain what different buttons do. In this activity, we will learn how to change the color of HTML elements.

STEP 1 – START A NEW HTML FILE ▷

⇨ Start your text editor, or click **File** > **New File**.

STEP 2 – ADD YOUR CODE ▷

⇨ Carefully type this into your text editor:

Sublime Text

```
1  <html>
2  <h1>Invitation List</h1>
3  <p style="color:red;">Alex</p>
4  <p style="color:green;">Anna</p>
5  <p style="color:blue;">Max</p>
6  </html>
```

Start the web page.
Add main heading.
Type very carefully, adding all quotes, colons, and semicolons.
End the web page.

STEP 3 – SAVE YOUR PAGE ▷

⇨ Click **File** > **Save**.

⇨ Browse to your **Documents** folder.

⇨ Type **colors.html** as the filename.

STEP 4 – VIEW YOUR PAGE ▷

⇨ Open your **Documents** folder and double-click the **colors.html** file.

Documents/colors.html
Invitation List
Alex
Anna
Max

 Now view your new web page!

◀ KEY CONCEPT

STYLE ATTRIBUTES

To tell the browser what color our text will be, we add extra information to the paragraph tags. This is done by adding a *style attribute* to the opening tag of the HTML element.

Remember the equals sign, double quotes, colons, and semicolon, as well as the angle brackets for the tags!

Style attribute   The value we want to give it
↓   ↙

< p style="color:red;">Alex</ p>

↑
The *property* we are setting
(Use sets of double quotes for properties.)

CUSTOMIZE

⇨ Now add more paragraphs with different names and different colors. Try out light or dark colors by adding the words **light** or **dark** to your code, such as **darkblue** or **lightgreen**.

⇨ Remember to click **File** > **Save** in the text editor, then *refresh* your browser.

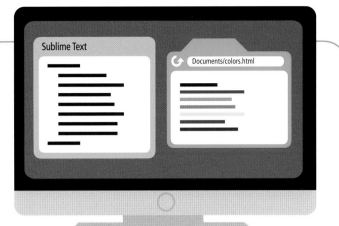

16 MILLION COLORS

There is another, more precise, way to set colors, that mixes together red, green, and blue light. A number is given between 0 and 255 for the amount of red, green, and blue in each color, giving more than 16 million combinations. This is called the *RGB* color system.

The code to show bright red is 255,0,0. The red value is 255, green is 0, and blue is 0. The RGB value is then converted into a special code called *hexadecimal*, which uses the letters A to F instead of 10 to 15. The hexadecimal code for red is: #FF0000.

Don't worry if you don't understand all that yet, just try using these color codes and experiment!

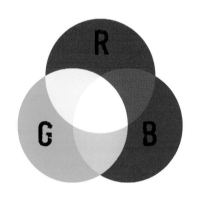

Hexadecimal codes must start with a hashtag # symbol. The letters of the code can be capital or lower case.

Color	Red	Green	Blue	Hex code
Red	255	0	0	FF0000
Green	0	255	0	00FF00
Blue	0	0	255	0000FF
Yellow	255	255	0	FFFF00
Purple	128	0	128	800080
White	255	255	255	FFFFFF
Black	0	0	0	000000
Dark Red	204	0	0	CC0000

⇨ Edit your text by changing the names and using hexadecimal values instead of color names.

Sublime Text

```
1  <html>
2  <h1>Invitation List</h1>
3  <p style="color:#FF8C00;">Jo</p>
4  <p style="color:#800080;">Maria</p>
5  <p style="color:#FFFF00;">Paul</p>
6  </html>
```

❯ PHOTOGRAPHS AND IMAGES

We've seen how color can be used to make web pages more interesting and informative. Images and photos are another important element used in web pages. To add photos to a web page, we need to use the image tag, **<img>**. We're going to create an animal web page, like the one below.

STEP 1 – PLANNING

⇨ Decide what images you would like to display on your web page. They can be photographs or other images. The example here uses *jpeg images* of a lion, an elephant, a dolphin, and a tiger. The names of these animals are used in the code later. It might help for you to use images of the same animals the first time you try this code. Then, you can switch it up by choosing your own animals.

Documents/photos.html

STEP 2 – FIND A AN IMAGE

⇨ Find the images you have decided to use by searching online. Use jpeg images and name the files. The filenames are important because they are used in the code later. We have named our images **lion.jpg**, **elephant.jpg**, **dolphin.jpg**, and **tiger.jpg**. Use these names if you are following this example. They need to be placed in the same folder as your HTML file. (See the copyright page for information about using other people's photos in your programs.)

STEP 3 – CHECK!

⇨ Open your **Documents** folder and check the image file is there.

⇨ If it is not there, go back to step 2 and try again.

STEP 4 – START A NEW HTML FILE

⇨ Carefully type this into your text editor:

Sublime Text	
1 `<html>`	Start the web page.
2 `<img src='lion.jpg'>`	Use image filename as the *URL*.
3 `</html>`	End the web page.

STEP 5 – SAVE YOUR PAGE

⇨ Click **File** > **Save**.

⇨ Save to your **Documents** folder.

⇨ Type **photos.html** as the filename. The **photos.html** file must be in the same **Documents** folder as your image.

STEP 6 – VIEW YOUR PAGE

⇨ Go to your **Documents** folder and double-click the **photos.html** file.

Documents/photos.html

If you type the code incorrectly or get the filename wrong, you may see this icon instead of the image. Check your code carefully. Save it again and refresh.

STEP 7 – MORE IMAGES

⇨ Repeat step 2 to add more images to your **Documents** folder. Repeat steps 3 to 5, adding the code to show your new images.

Sublime Text

```
1  <html>
2  <img src='lion.jpg'>
3  <img src='elephant.jpg'>
4  <img src='dolphin.jpg'>
5  <img src='tiger.jpg'>
6  </html>
```

Start the web page.

Add the **img tags** for your new images one at a time.

End the web page.

 Save and **Refresh** to see your page of images.

 **KEY CONCEPT**

IMAGES

To add photos and images to a web page, we need to use the image tag, `<img>`. The image tag is unusual, as it has no closing tag.

img tag

The **src** attribute is short for **source**—where to find the image.

`<img src='lion.jpg'>`

NOTE: Single quotes are used to indicate where an element can be found.

The **URL** must have single quotes around it.

The **filename** has two parts: the name (**lion**) and its type (**jpg**).

⟩ STYLE AND CSS

You now know how to add the basic elements of text and images to a web page. Let's have another look at how to change the appearance of multiple elements on the page, using a couple of lines of code. This gives a polished look to your page and makes your code more reliable and adaptable.

STEP 1 – PLANNING

Documents/stylish.html

⇨ Decide how you would like to present your images.

⇨ Think about adding borders and using different colors in the style section.

STEP 2 – OPEN PHOTOS.HTML

⇨ You will need your file from page 11: **photos.html**.

⇨ Open your text editor and browse to find the file.

⇨ Click **File** > **Save As** and rename the file **stylish.html**

STEP 3 – CHECK IT

⇨ Open your **Documents** folder. Find the new **stylish.html** file and double-click on it. Check that your new file appears in the browser.

⇨ Arrange your screen in the usual way with the text editor on the left and browser on the right.

STYLE SHEETS

The code language we use to say what goes on a web page is called HTML. The language we use to describe how these elements will look on the screen is called *CSS*. CSS stands for **Cascading Style Sheets**. There are three main ways we can use CSS:

- **Inline styling** where we put the styling information inside the opening tag of paragraph elements (see page 8)

- **Internal Style Sheets** where we put the styling information within the web page (see page 13)

- **External Style Sheets** allows you to change the appearance of the whole site by changing just one file. This is a separate file that each page has a link to.

STEP 4 – ADD A STYLE SECTION ▷

⇨ Put the cursor after **<html>** and press enter a few times to make some space. Insert the code highlighted below. This will give all the images a solid black border, *8 pixels* thick. They will also have a *margin* of 8 pixels around them and they will be 90 pixels high. Sublime text should automatically create indents for you, but if it does not, remember to indent lines of code exactly as shown here.

Sublime Text

```
1  <html>
2  <style>
3      img{border:8px solid black;
4      margin:8px; height:90px;}
5      body{background-color:orange;}
6  </style>
7  <img src='lion.jpg'>
8  <img src='elephant.jpg'>
9  <img src='dolphin.jpg'>
10 <img src='tiger.jpg'>
11 </html>
```

Start the style section.

Add an image border of 8 pixels, a margin of 8 pixels, and make the images 90 pixels high.

Add an orange background color to the page.

End the style section.

⇨ You must type the code very carefully, using the curly brackets { }, semicolons, and colons. It doesn't matter if you press enter or not after each of the semicolons.

STEP 5 – TEST IT ▷

⇨ Click **File** > **Save** in the text editor, then **Refresh** your browser.

 View your web page. Does it look similar to the illustration at the beginning of page 12?

CUSTOMIZE

• Try changing the colors used in the style section.

• Vary the size of the margin and the image height.

• Use dotted or dashed lines instead of solid lines for the border.

• Add some paragraphs to label the photos. Set the color of these by adding p{color:blue;} to the style section.

A pixel is a an image element—one of millions of tiny grid squares used to create an image onscreen.

 KEY CONCEPT

STYLE

Use a **<style>** section to include some **CSS**. This will set the look of multiple elements on the page, without you having to repeat the code again.

› LINKING IT TOGETHER

We get to another page of a book by simply turning the page. On the web, pages are linked to other pages by *hyperlinks*, or *links* for short. On the web, we either type in a new address or click on one of these links.

STEP 1 – START A NEW HTML FILE ▷

⇨ Carefully type this into your text editor. In step 3, link to your favorite website, such as National Geographic Kids.

	Sublime Text	
1	<html>	
2	<h1>My Links</h1>	Add a simple heading.
3	<a href='http://kids.nationalgeographic.com'>National Geographic Kids</a>	Start the anchor tag <a. Then add href to set the URL and link to your favorite website.
4	 	Add a line break ** **. It starts a new line in
5	<a href='http://www.youtube.com'>Youtube</a>	Link to Youtube. the browser, leaving a gap between links.
6	 	Add a line break ** **.
7	</html>	

⇨ Save your page in the **Documents** folder.

⇨ Type **links.html** as the filename.

STEP 2 – TEST YOUR PAGE ▷

⇨ Go to your **Documents** folder and double-click the **links.html** file.

⇨ Click to test each **link**. It should jump to the website shown.

Documents/links.html

My Links

National Geographic Kids
YouTube

⇨ Click the **back button** to return to your page.

⇨ Web pages don't use only text as links—many also use an icon or image. To use an image as a link:

Sublime Text

```
1   <html>
2   <h1>My Links</h1>
3   <a href='http://kids.nationalgeographic.com'>
    National Geographic Kids</a>
4   <br>
5   <a href='http://www.youtube.com'>Youtube</a>
6   <br>
7   <a href='http://zoo.sandiegozoo.org'>
8   <img src='lion.jpg'>
9   </a>
10  </html>
```

⇨ Click before the last line **</html>** and press enter a few times to make some space.

⇨ Add all the code highlighted in green.

⇨ Instead of using text as the link, use one of the images you downloaded on page 10.

⇨ **Save** the page and **Refresh** your browser.

CUSTOMIZE

- Create groups of links, such as links to information about one of your hobbies. Use subheadings to label them.
- Add a style section to the web page and change the appearance of the images you use and the background.

Documents/links.html

My Links

National Geographic Kids
YouTube

 When you click on the image of the lion, it should take you to the San Diego Zoo's website.

 KEY CONCEPT

USING HYPERLINKS

The link starts with an opening anchor tag **<a>**.

The link ends with a closing anchor tag **</a>**.

`<a href='http://www.youtube.com'>YouTube</a>`

The **href** attribute is used to set the URL the link will jump to.

The **URL** (address) is typed here between the quotes.

The text for the link to display.

› INPUT ELEMENTS

In addition to showing information, many web pages ask the user to enter various details. In this activity, we will look at different forms of *input* elements that ask for information. Our site won't be online and it won't save any information, so don't worry about what you type in during this activity.

STEP 1 – PLANNING

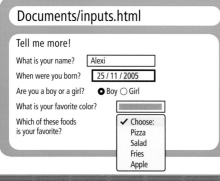

Documents/inputs.html

Tell me more!

What is your name? `Alexi`
When were you born? `25 / 11 / 2005`
Are you a boy or a girl? ● Boy ○ Girl
What is your favorite color? ▬▬▬
Which of these foods is your favorite?
✓ Choose:
Pizza
Salad
Fries
Apple

⇨ Decide which questions you want to ask visitors to your web page.

STEP 2 – START A NEW HTML FILE

⇨ Carefully type this into your text editor:

Sublime Text

```
1  <html>
2  <h2>Tell me more!</h2>
3  <label>What is your name?</label>
4  <input type="text">
5  </html>
```

Add the basic text input box. It has no closing tag.

Add a heading.

Add a label. This is similar to the paragraph element, but the next element will still be on the same line.

⇨ Save your page in the **Documents** folder.

⇨ Type **inputs.html** as the filename.

STEP 3 – TEST YOUR PAGE

⇨ Double-click the **inputs.html** file in your **Documents** folder.

The user adds their name here.

Documents/welcome.html

Tell me more!

What is your name? [   ]

CUSTOMIZE

- Think of more questions to add. Which type of input would be best for each one?
- Add a style section.

⇨ Here is the code for the whole page. Click before **</html>** and press enter to make some space. Try adding the code one input element at a time, then **Save** and test each time.

```
Sublime Text
1   <html>
2      <h2>Tell me more!</h2>

3      <label>What is your name?</label>
4      <input type="text">
5      <br><br>

6      <label>When were you born?</label>
7      <input type="date">
8      <br><br>

9      <label>Are you a boy or a girl?</label>
10     <input type="radio" name="bg">Boy
11     <input type="radio" name="bg">Girl
12     <br><br>

13     <label>What is your favorite color?</label>
14     <input type="color">
15     <br><br>

16     <label>Which of these foods is your favorite?</label>
17     <select>
18        <option>Choose:</option>
19        <option>Pizza</option>
20        <option>Salad</option>
21        <option>Fries</option>
22        <option>Apple</option>
23     </select>
24  </html>
```

Add a blank line with a double **
** element. This gap just makes our code clearer!

Set up a **date picker**, which contains a list of dates to choose from.

Add a **radio button**. It is a good type of input to use if there are only a limited number of choices. The code **name="bg"** links the two options together.

Set up a **color picker**, which contains different colors to choose from. Each browser will present this differently.

Create a **drop-down menu**.

Add options for the drop-down menu.

Add a closing tag for the drop-down.

 Save and **Refresh** to see your web page. Ask a friend to answer the questions.

INDENTING
Each paragraph in a book is usually indented. Text editors often automatically indent parts of your code to make it easier to read (see the last section of code above). If the lines do not automatically indent, be sure to indent the lines yourself, exactly as shown.

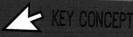 **KEY CONCEPT**

INPUT AND SELECT ELEMENTS
There are a variety of **input elements** that can be used to get information from the person viewing a web page. Another way is to use a **select element** by creating a **drop-down menu**.

LINKING AND EMBEDDING VIDEO

You may want to add videos to your web pages. Linking to a video on another website is one way to do this, but then your website users will be directed away from your page. The best way to keep users on your page is to *embed* the video.

Some videos (particularly music videos) will look as though they are embedded, but when you click them they will act as a link. This is just how the video owners have asked the video to be *hosted*.

STEP 1 – PLANNING

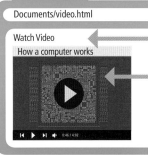

Documents/video.html

Watch Video
How a computer works

This is a **hyperlink** (see page 15) that links to the page with the video on it.

This is the same video, but **embedded** on the web page within an **<iframe>**.

LINKING TO A VIDEO

STEP 2 – GET THE VIDEO URL

⇨ Choose a video from YouTube or a similar website.

www.youtube.com/watch=v

www.youtube.com/watch=v

⇨ Click the **URL** in the address bar at the top. Make sure it is all highlighted.

⇨ Right-click on the URL.

| Cut |
| **Copy** |
| Paste |

⇨ Click **Copy**.

STEP 3 – START A NEW HTML FILE

Sublime Text

```
1  <html>
2  <a href='https://www.youtube.com/watch?v=J8hzJxb0rpc'>
3  Watch Video
4  </a>
5  </html>
```

Click **Edit > Paste** to add the URL.
(**Don't try to type it in!**)

Remember to close the link with **</a>** and **</html>** to show the end of the page.

⇨ Click **File > Save**.   ⇨ **Save** to **Documents**.   ⇨ Type **video.html** as the filename.

STEP 4 – TEST

⇨ Double-click the **video.html** file in your **Documents** folder.

Documents/video.html

Watch Video

⇨ Click the link and you should jump to the page with your chosen video.

CUSTOMIZE

• Find another video and click **Share**. Before you copy the embed code, try experimenting with the options that set the size of the video.

• Add other elements, such as headings and titles, to the page.

• Add a style section to add color to the page.

EMBEDDING A VIDEO

STEP I – GET THE EMBED CODE

⇨ Choose a video from YouTube or another similar website.

Share

⇨ Click the **Share** button. (Look in the middle, below the video.)

Embed

⇨ Click the **Embed** button.

llowfullscreen></iframe>

⇨ Right-click the embed code.

⇨ Click **Copy**.

STEP 2 – START A NEW HTML

⇨ Add **<html>** then press **enter**. **</html>** shows the end of the HTML.

⇨ Click **Edit > Paste** to add the embed code. You will see that the embed code includes **<iframe>** and **</iframe>**.

```
Sublime Text
1  <html>
2  <iframe width="560" height="315"
3  src="https://www.youtube.com/embed/J8hzJxb0rpc?rel=0
4  &amp;controls=0&amp;showinfo=0" frameborder="0"
5  allowfullscreen></iframe>
6  </html>
```

⇨ Click **File > Save**.

⇨ Save to **Documents**.

⇨ Type **video2.html** as the filename.

STEP 3 – TEST

⇨ Double-click the **video2.html** file in your **Documents** folder.

Documents/video2.html

How a computer works

 Your video should now appear, embedded in your own web page. Try playing it!

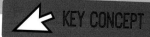 **KEY CONCEPT**

IFRAMES

iframes can be used to include content, such as videos, from another site on your own web page.

› FAVORITE MOVIE CLIPS

In this program, you will use iframes and embedded video to create a page of your favorite movie clips or trailers. Use headings and paragraphs to label each clip and add a style section to make the page look really cool. You could even try adding a special background to the page.

STEP 1 – PLANNING

Documents/movieclips.html

My Favorite Movie Trailers

Cartoons

Action movies

Make a bold heading, changing the color and font.

Find videos of your favorite movie trailers. Embed each video in an iframe. Use the style section to give all iframes a border and margin.

Use <h2> or <h3> subheadings for different groups of movie clips. You might choose to arrange your movie clips by genre of movie. We have used cartoons and action movies here.

Use a **background image**, instead of a color only, to make the page look amazing!

You could use **inline style** to give each subheading a different color.

STEP 2 – USING A BACKGROUND IMAGE

We have looked at how to set the background color (see page 13) and how to download images to use in a web page. You can also combine these techniques to set a background image for the whole page.

⇨ Find a file you want to use—try an image search for **background textures**.

⇨ Right-click and **Save** the file.

⇨ Make a style section in your HTML and add in this code:

Type the name of your file here. Remember the quotes.

```
body{background-image: url('my-bg.png');}
```

Type the letters url as well as the filename of the background image.

⇨ Make sure you include all the code: the curly brackets { }, colon, normal brackets, and semicolon.

⇨ Start your text editor and click **File** > **New File**.

⇨ Here is the code for the whole page. Rather than typing it all in at once, start with both HTML tags, then the headings. After that, copy an embed code for one video (see page 18) and try pasting it in. Save it as **movieclips.html**. Preview and test your file in your browser.

Sublime Text

```
1   <html>

2   <style>
3       body{background-image: url('my-bg.png');}
4       h1{font-family:Tahoma; margin:20px;}
5       h2{font-family:Tahoma; margin:20px;}
6       iframe{margin:20px; border:black solid 20px;}
7   </style>

8   <h1>My Favorite Movie Trailers</h1>
9   <iframe ...></iframe>
10  <iframe ...></iframe>

11  <h2 style='color:Green;'>Cartoons</h2>
12  <iframe ...></iframe>
13  <iframe ...></iframe>

14  <h2 style='color:Magenta;'>Action movies</h2>
15  <iframe ...></iframe>

16  </html>
```

Start the style section.
Set the page background.

Choose a font and margin size for your headings ("20px" means 20 pixels).

Add this style to **iframe** to give each video a black border around it.

Add the main heading.

Paste your two movie trailers here (one on each line). Copy the embed code (see page 19) from the video website and paste it in place of the highlighted code.

Add inline styling for each **<h2>** heading.

Paste your cartoon movie clips here (one on each line). Paste the embed codes in place of the highlighted code.

Add inline styling for each **<h2>** heading.

Paste your action movie clip here. Paste the embed code in place of the highlighted code.
Remember to close the web page with **</html>**.

 Keep saving and refreshing to test your code as you are typing it in.

CUSTOMIZE

- Use all the techniques you have learned so far to make the page look just as you want it!

- Change colors, fonts, and sizes, or add other images.

 **KEY CONCEPT**

FONT FAMILY

You can choose the font a paragraph or heading element uses. CSS calls this setting the **font-family**.

p{font-family: Arial;}
p{font-family: 'Times New Roman';}

Use quotes if the font has any spaces in its name.

> IMAGE GALLERY

We have looked at how to make images into links (see page 15). We will extend this idea by creating an image gallery. Your image gallery could have any theme, but we will use famous landmarks as our focus in this activity.

STEP 1 – PLANNING

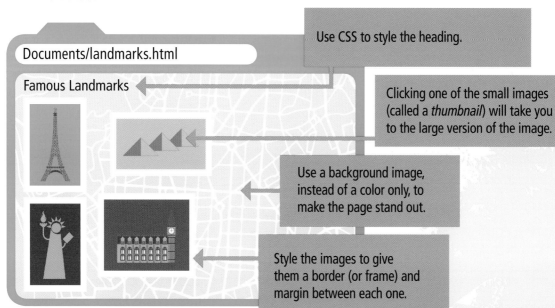

Documents/landmarks.html

Famous Landmarks

Use CSS to style the heading.

Clicking one of the small images (called a *thumbnail*) will take you to the large version of the image.

Use a background image, instead of a color only, to make the page stand out.

Style the images to give them a border (or frame) and margin between each one.

STEP 2 – GET THE URL OF AN IMAGE ▶

You need to choose an image to use. However, instead of downloading the image, you need to copy the URL (address) of the image on the website.

When you write your code, repeat these steps for three more images, one at a time. You will place each image URL in different lines of code, as shown on page 23.

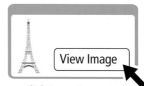

⇨ Go online and search for an image of the Eiffel Tower.

⇨ Choose an image and click it.

⇨ Click it again to get a larger version. If you see a **View Image** button, click it.

⇨ Right-click the image.

⇨ Click **Copy Image Address**.

⇨ Start your text editor or click **File** > **New File**.

⇨ Here is the code for the whole page. Rather than typing it all in at once, start with both HTML tags, then the headings. After that, copy an embed code for one image and try pasting it in. Save it as **landmarks.html**. Preview and test your file in your browser. See page 14 for help with making links.

Sublime Text

```
1   <html>

2   <style>
3       h1{font-family: Verdana;}
4       body{background-image: url('bg1.png');}
5       img{margin:10px; height:160px;
6           border:20px solid white;}
7   </style>

8   <h1>Famous Landmarks</h1>

9   <a href='PASTE IMAGE1 URL'>
10      <img src='PASTE IMAGE1 URL'>
11  </a>

12  <a href='PASTE IMAGE2 URL'>
13      <img src='PASTE IMAGE2 URL'>
14  </a>

15  <a href='PASTE IMAGE3 URL'>
16          <img src='PASTE IMAGE3 URL'>
17  </a>

18  <a href='PASTE IMAGE4 URL'>
19          <img src='PASTE IMAGE4 URL'>
20  </a>

21  </html>
```

Start the style section.

Set the page background (see page 20).

Choose the margin between each image. Set the height to 160px so all images line up nicely. The white 20px border will look like a picture frame.

Type **<a href='** . Next paste in the image URL you copied in step 1. Then type **'>**.

Type **<img src='** . Then paste in the image URL and type **'>**.

Type **</a>** to close the link.

Repeat these three lines of code for each of the other images in your gallery. Each time, copy and paste the URL of the image.

Remember to close the web page with **</html>**.

CUSTOMIZE

- Experiment with different colors, fonts, and sizes.

- Add sections to your page. Try adding subheadings for each continent that the landmarks are found in.

Save and test your code after adding each image. Look up and down the text editor for patterns in your code to keep it *bug*-free.

GEOGRAPHY QUIZ

There are many ways you can build a quiz using HTML. We are going to make our quiz really interesting by using some *animation* to reveal the answer. There is a special feature of CSS that allows us to change a property, such as color, to create animation. We can also use this feature to make the answer spin and reveal itself slowly.

STEP 1 – PLANNING

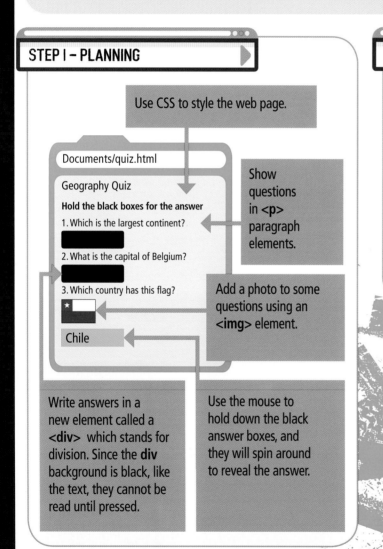

Use CSS to style the web page.

Documents/quiz.html

Geography Quiz

Hold the black boxes for the answer

1. Which is the largest continent?

2. What is the capital of Belgium?

3. Which country has this flag?

Chile

Show questions in **\<p\>** paragraph elements.

Add a photo to some questions using an **\<img\>** element.

Write answers in a new element called a **\<div\>** which stands for division. Since the **div** background is black, like the text, they cannot be read until pressed.

Use the mouse to hold down the black answer boxes, and they will spin around to reveal the answer.

STEP 2 – DOWNLOAD IMAGES

⇨ Decide on a topic for the quiz. In this example we will use geography, but you could choose something else.

Chilean flag   Search

⇨ Search for any photos you need.

⇨ Right-click one image.

⇨ Click **Save Image As**.

⇨ Navigate to your **Documents** folder, then click **Save**.

CUSTOMIZE

• Add more questions. A good quiz needs at least ten.

• Include more images for some questions.

• Make a multiple choice question with several possible answers.

• Experiment with different color values for the **div:active** section.

• Alter the value **1800** to **180** or **3600**. What changes when you press an answer div?

⇨ Start your text editor, or click **File** > **New File**.

⇨ Here is the code for the whole page. Type in the HTML tags and the style section, followed by the first question. Save your code as **quiz.html**, then open it in your browser and test it. If it works, add the remaining questions one at a time.

Sublime Text

```
1   <html>

2   <style>
3       body{margin:20px;
4           background-color:lightblue;}
5       p{font-size:16px;}
6       div{
7           background-color:black;
8           width:120px; height:40px;
9           text-align:center;
10          line-height:40px;
11          font-size:16px;
12          transition:all 2s;}

13      div:active{
14          background-color:lightgreen;
14          transform:rotate(1800deg);}
16  </style>

17  <h1>Geography Quiz</h1>
18  <h3>Hold the black boxes for the answer</h3>

19  <p>1. Which is the largest continent?</p>
20  <div>Asia</div>

21  <p>2. What is the capital of Belgium?</p>
22  <div>Brussels</div>

23  <p>3. Which country has this flag?</p>
24  <img src='chile_flag.png'>
25  <br>
26  <div>Chile</div>

27  </html>
```

Start the style section.

Put some space around all elements with a 20 pixel margin.

Add background color for the page.

Add the font size for the questions.

Add the div element to hold the answers.

Add the div's starting color.
Add the div's starting size.
Center the answer text in the div.

Animate the div smoothly over two seconds if the div changes any of its properties.

Define the div when it is active and the mouse is pressed on it.

Turn the div green.

Rotate the div 1800 degrees (five complete rotations).

Use a **<p>** for each question and a **<div>** for the answer.

Add **<img>** after the **<p>** for any images you want to include.

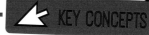
Now view your web page!

KEY CONCEPTS

ACTIVE

• When the mouse is pressed down over an element, you define properties for that element by using the **:active** code. In this activity, **div** is the element that reveals the answer when the mouse is pressed over it.

TRANSITION

• The **code transition** makes specific properties change slowly. In this activity, the **div** reveals its answer slowly, like an animation.

❯ PIZZA DELIVERY

We have seen how input elements can be used to let users enter information on a web page (page 16). In this program, we will apply those techniques to create a web page to order your own perfect pizza. (You will have to cook it yourself, though!)

(page 16)

STEP 1 – PLANNING

Style the page with CSS.

Use a photo of a pizza in an **<img>** element.

Use **radio buttons** to let people select which type of pizza crust they want.

Use a **drop-down menu** to select the type of cheese.

Choose additional toppings with **checkboxes**.

Documents/pizza.html

Max's Pizza Shop

Delivery

Choose your crust:

- ⦿ Classic
- ⦿ Cheese
- ⦿ Crispy

Cheese type:

Mozzarella ⬍

Toppings:

☑ Ham   ☐ Peppers   ☑ Mushrooms

STEP 2 – FIND A PHOTO

⇨ Download a photo of a pizza into your **Documents** folder.

⇨ Search for a pizza photo.   ⇨ Right-click one photo.   ⇨ Click **Save Image As** and name it pizza.jpg.   ⇨ Navigate to your **Documents** folder, then click **Save**.

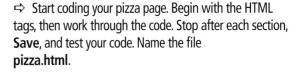

⇨ Start your text editor, or click **File** > **New File**.

Sublime Text

```
1   <html>
2   <style>
3       body{font-size:14px;
4           font-family:Arial;
5           background-color:red;
6           margin:40px;}
7   </style>

8   <h1 style='color:white'>Max's Pizza Shop</h1>
9   <img width="300" src="pizza.jpg">
10  <h3>Delivery</h3>

11  <p>Choose your base:</p>
12  <input name="base" type="radio">Classic<br>
13  <input name="base" type="radio">Cheese<br>
14  <input name="base" type="radio">Crispy<br>

15  <br>

16  <p>Cheese type:</p>
17  <select style="font-size: 24px;">
18          <option>Mozzarella</option>
19          <option>Cheddar</option>
20          <option>No cheese</option>
21  </select>

22  <p>Toppings:</p>
23  <input type="checkbox"> Ham
24  <input type="checkbox"> Peppers
25  <input type="checkbox"> Mushrooms
26  </html>
```

⇨ Start coding your pizza page. Begin with the HTML tags, then work through the code. Stop after each section, **Save**, and test your code. Name the file **pizza.html**.

Start the style section.

Add styling in the body section. Most of the input elements will pick up this styling, too. To make it clearer to read your code, press **enter** after each semicolon.

Use inline styling to set the color for the heading.

Use the **picture** downloaded from step 1. Adjust the width if necessary.

Set the name of each radio button input to be the same. This makes sure only one can be selected.

Start a new line.

Add a select element for the drop-down menu to choose the cheese. Each type of cheese needs a new option element.

Add a **checkbox** input element for each additional topping. This will let the person using the web page tick one or more options. The radio button only lets you select one.

Now view your web page!

CUSTOMIZE
- Spend some time trying out different color, font, and size changes in the style section.
- Add extra toppings and some more photos to show the different toppings available.
- Add a text input box to allow people to type in any extra requests.
- Create another heading and section on the page for drinks.
- Look for a suitable image to use as a background for the page.

SPORTS MINI-SITE

In this program, you are going to learn how to make a mini website. Rather than just one page, you will build several pages with information about different sports, and one index page that will contain links to each of the individual sports pages.

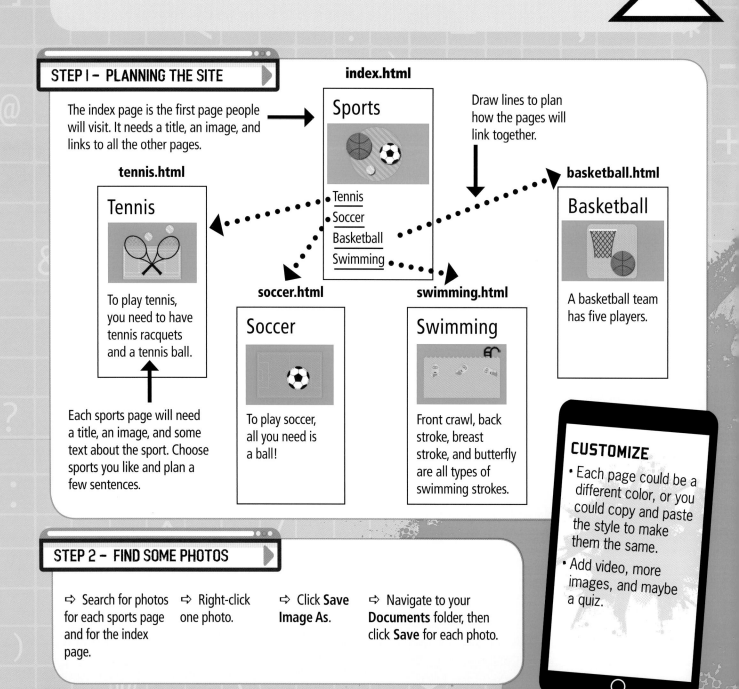

STEP 1 – PLANNING THE SITE

The index page is the first page people will visit. It needs a title, an image, and links to all the other pages.

index.html

Sports

- Tennis
- Soccer
- Basketball
- Swimming

Draw lines to plan how the pages will link together.

tennis.html

Tennis

To play tennis, you need to have tennis racquets and a tennis ball.

Each sports page will need a title, an image, and some text about the sport. Choose sports you like and plan a few sentences.

soccer.html

Soccer

To play soccer, all you need is a ball!

swimming.html

Swimming

Front crawl, back stroke, breast stroke, and butterfly are all types of swimming strokes.

basketball.html

Basketball

A basketball team has five players.

CUSTOMIZE
- Each page could be a different color, or you could copy and paste the style to make them the same.
- Add video, more images, and maybe a quiz.

STEP 2 – FIND SOME PHOTOS

⇨ Search for photos for each sports page and for the index page.

⇨ Right-click one photo.

⇨ Click **Save Image As**.

⇨ Navigate to your **Documents** folder, then click **Save** for each photo.

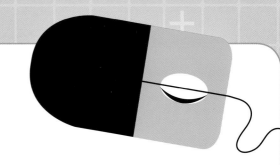

STEP 3 – START THE INDEX PAGE ▷

⇨ Carefully type this code to start your index page:

Sublime Text

```
1 <html>
2 <h1>Sports</h1>
3 <img src='sport.png' width='200'><br>
4 <a href='tennis.html'>Tennis</a> <br>
5 <a href='soccer.html'>Soccer</a> <br>
6 <a href='basketball.html'>Basketball</a> <br>
7 <a href='swimming.html'>Swimming</a>
8 </html>
```

Add a main heading.

Use the image from step 2.

Each page will need its own link. Use **<a>** tags, typing the filename as the value for the href attribute. Type the name of the sport before the closing tag **</a>**. Use **
** tags to make each link start on a new line.

⇨ Save the page as **index.html**. Find it in your **Documents** folder and double-click it to see how it looks. Try clicking one of the links. You will get an error saying **Your file was not found**, so we need to start building these other pages.

⇨ Click the **back button** to return to your index.

STEP 4 – START THE TENNIS PAGE ▷

⇨ Carefully type this code to start the tennis page:

Sublime Text

```
1 <html>
2 <h1>Tennis</h1>
3 <img src='tennis-game.jpg'>
4 <p>To play tennis, you need to have tennis
  racquets and a tennis ball.</p>
5 </html>
```

KEY CONCEPT

WEBSITES AND RELATIVE LINKS

Websites are multiple pages linked together with **a** tags. We use **relative links** to do this, by typing the file name without **http** or any web address. This is because all pages and files will be in the same folder.

Use the name of the tennis photo from step 2.

Use a **<p> tag**, then start typing what you know about tennis. You can always add more text later. Don't worry if it spills over the edge of the page.

 Save the page as **tennis.html**. In your browser, try clicking the link to **Tennis**. It should now take you to your new page!

STEP 5 – MORE PAGES ▷

⇨ Repeat step 4 for each of the other sports. Type the name of the photo files carefully. After you complete each page, save it with the name of the sport followed by **.html,** then test your index page again.

> GLOSSARY

ANIMATION Making elements on a web page move, or fade in or out

ATTRIBUTE Extra information about an HTML element, such as the address of an image

BROWSER A program used to view web pages, such as Chrome or Internet Explorer

BUG An error in a web page that stops it displaying correctly

COPYRIGHT Rules and laws protecting the person who created an image or piece of work

CSS (CASCADING STYLE SHEETS) The language used to describe how HTML elements will look

DEBUG Removing bugs (or errors) from an HTML page

DOCUMENTS FOLDER One of the main folders used to store files on a computer

ELEMENT One of the objects making up a web page, such as a paragraph or an image

EMBEDDING Placing an element on one web page, but getting its content from a different website

HEXADECIMAL A system of numbers based on 16s, using digits from 0 to 9, then A to F

HOST To be accessed by, or made available to, the public

HTML (HYPERTEXT MARKUP LANGUAGE) The language used to build web pages

INPUT A way to get information into a web page or computer

JPEG/JPG IMAGE A type of image format, usually found online

LINK/HYPERLINK A clickable link from one web page to another

MARGIN The space around an HTML element

PIXEL A small dot on the screen; it can be used as a unit of measurement

PROPERTY Information about the style of an element, such as its color or size

REFRESH To load a web page again in the browser, so changes to the page can be seen

RGB The system used to mix red, green, and blue light to make any color

STYLE Information written in CSS describing things such as the size and color of an element

TAGS Special words in an HTML document surrounded by angle brackets <> defining an element

TEXT EDITOR A program used to create and change text, such as the code used to build a web page

THUMBNAIL A small image that links to a larger image when clicked

URL (UNIFORM RESOURCE LOCATOR) The address of a file on the web

WEB STANDARDS
Modern web browsers will still show parts of your HTML, even if there are bugs in it. However, you should try to code everything correctly because errors can creep in.

Once you start to publish your web pages, you will need to check if your code works on other browsers (see page 4) and on different screen sizes.

BUGS AND DEBUGGING

When you find your code is not working as expected, stop and look through each command you have put in. Think about what you want it to do, and what it is really telling the computer to do. If you are entering one of the programs in this book, check that you have not missed a line. Here are some things to watch for:

Use tags correctly:

```
<h1>A
<h1>B
<h1>C
```
✗

```
<h1>A</h1>
<h1>B</h1>
<h1>C</h1>
```
✓

Most elements need an opening and a closing tag.

Use tags correctly:

```
<p>Line 1
Line 2
Line 3</p>
```
✗

```
<p>Line 1</p>
<p>Line 2</p>
<p>Line 3</p>
```
✓

Typing **enter** in your code won't start a new line on your web page.

Close tags:

```
<p>Hello<p>
```
✗

```
<p>Hello</p>
```
✓

Closing tags need a **forward slash** symbol.

Be careful with quotes:

```
<p style="color:red;>Pizza</p>
```
✗

```
<p style="color:red';>Pizza</p>
```
✗

```
<p style="color:red;>"Pizza</p>
```
✗

```
<p style="color:red;">Pizza</p>
```
✓

Quotes always work in pairs. Make sure they match and are in the correct place.

Check URLs:

```
<a href='pgae2.htlm'>
```
✗

```
<a href='page2.html'>
```
✓

Type all URLs carefully and check that they are correct.

Type commands carefully:

```
<imge sorc='pic.png'>
```
✗

```
<img src='pic.png'>
```
✓

Make sure you spell tags correctly.

TIPS TO REDUCE BUGS

If you are making your own web page, spend time drawing a diagram and planning it before you start. Try changing values if things don't work, and don't be afraid to start again—you will learn from it.

Practice *debugging*! Make a very simple web page and get a friend to change one line of code while you're not looking. Can you fix it?

When things are working properly, spend time looking through your code so you understand each line. Experiment and change your code, and try out different values. To be good at debugging, you need to understand what each line of your code does and how it works.

INDEX